WORLD DISASTERS!

FLOOD

BRIAN KNAPP

Steck-Vaughn
L I B R A R Y

Austin, Texas

Published in the United States in 1990 by Steck-Vaughn Co., Austin, Texas, a subsidiary of National Education Corportation

© Earthscape Editions 1989
© Macmillan Publishers Limited 1989

First published in 1989
by Macmillan Children's Books
A division of Macmillan Publishers Ltd

Designed and produced by Earthscape Editions, Sonning Common, Oxon, England

Cover design by Julian Holland

Illustrations by
Duncan McCrae and Tim Smith

Printed and bound in the United States.

1 2 3 4 5 6 7 8 9 0 LB 94 93 92 91 90

Photographic credits

t = top b = bottom l-left r = right

All photographs are from the Earthscape Editions photographic library except for the following: contents page 31, 32, AOIS; 22 Cambridge University Collection; 11b Denver Post, 29t, 30b Prof. D.E. Walling; 7 Frank Lane Picture Agency; 29b, 35 OXFAM; 13bl, 14br, 15 Poppertoto; 36 Thames Water; 37 USDA: 10, 26, 33 USGA

Cover: Kent and Donna Danner/Science Photo Library
Flooding resulting from the breakage of Lawn Lake Dam in the Rocky Mountain National Park, Colorado

Library of Congress Cataloging-in-Publication Data

Knapp, Brian J.
   Flood/Brian Knapp.
      p.   cm. — (World disasters)
   Summary: Describes some of the world's great flood disasters, why floods occur, and how people have learned to live with floods.
      Includes index.
      ISBN 0-8114-2374-3
      1. Floods—Juvenile literature.   [1. Floods.]
I. Title   II. Series.
   GB1399.K63 1989
   363.3'493—dc20   89-11437
                                                                  CIP
                                                                  AC

Note to the reader
In this book there are some words in the text that are printed in **bold** type. This shows that the word is listed in the glossary on page 46. The glossary gives a brief explanation of words that may be new to you.

Contents

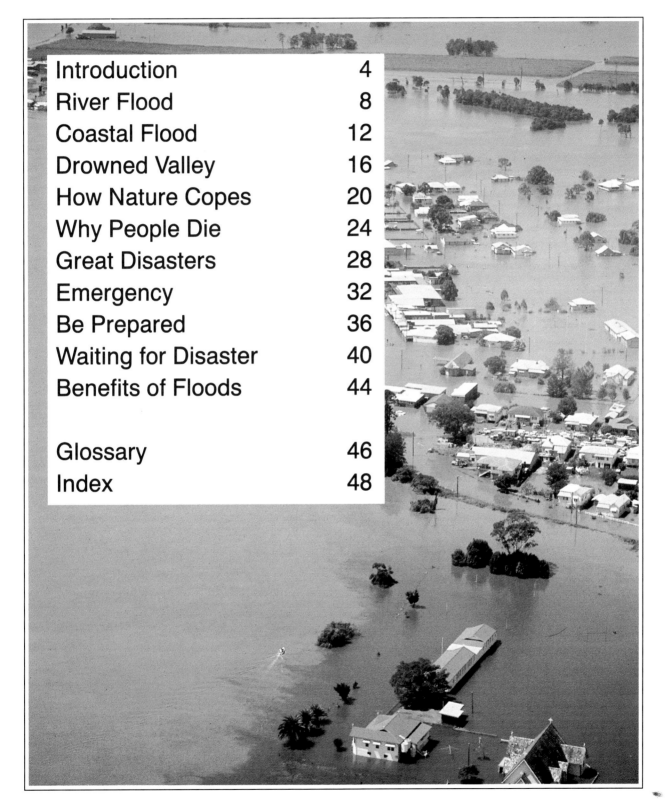

Introduction

A **flood** occurs when water spills either from a river channel or from the ocean over land that is normally dry. Many people who live on flat land near rivers or the ocean have their homes flooded quite regularly. However, although most floods cause little damage and inconvenience, from time to time there is a really large flood. Then many lives and much property are at risk and the flood may turn into a **disaster.**

In this book we will look at some of the world's great flood disasters and how people have learned to live with floods. To understand why flood disasters happen and how to be prepared for them, first we have to know a little about the part played by floods in the natural world.

The way water moves

Water can be found everywhere in the world. Some of it is locked up deep within the Earth and only released during **volcanic eruptions.** All the Earth's 3 billion cubic miles of water has been produced in this way. About 97 percent of the surface water is found in the oceans, and most of the rest is locked up in ice sheets and ice caps. Only a small proportion of the world's water is found in rivers and lakes, or in the soil and rocks. A little of the world's total water also occurs as a gas, making up the moisture in the air.

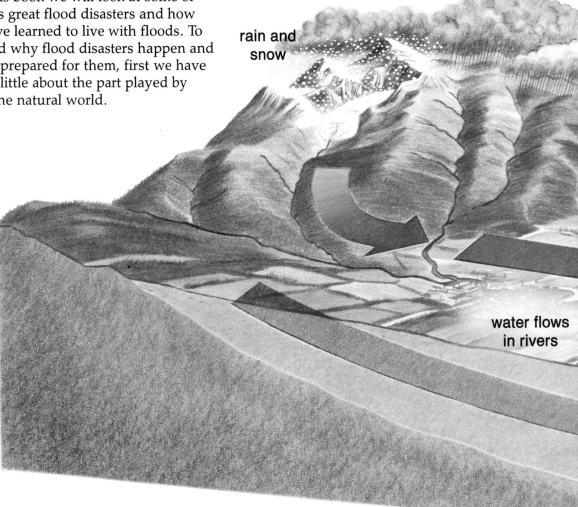

rain and snow

water flows in rivers

▲ *This diagram shows the way water moves from oceans, through clouds and rain, to rivers, and back to the oceans to complete the water cycle.*

The water cycle

The source of most rain is ocean water. As the sun shines on the ocean, it warms the surface and causes some of the water to **evaporate** and become **moisture** in the air. About 100,000 cubic miles of water evaporates from the oceans each year. The moisture is carried upward by air currents and it cools. When the moist air cools it can hold less water and some of the moisture forms into water droplets or snowflakes. When this happens clouds are produced.

Most rain falls back into the oceans and only about 10,000 cubic miles falls on land. The first part of any rain is used up in making the ground surface wet. After this rain begins to sink into the soil. The soil is like a sponge, containing many small passageways called pores that allow water to seep from the surface. Some water is held back in the pores and provides the moisture that plants need when there is little rain. The surplus water seeps deeper into the soil and possibly into the rocks beneath. In this

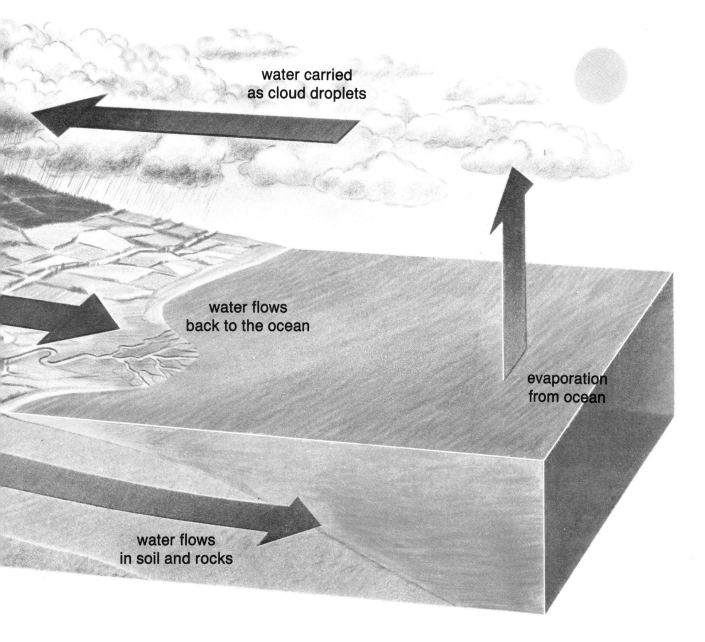

water carried
as cloud droplets

water flows
back to the ocean

evaporation
from ocean

water flows
in soil and rocks

way the soil and rock soak up the surplus water and only release it again slowly. It may take weeks or even months for water to reach the rivers through the soil and rock. In this way the soil and rock help to even out the flow of water to rivers, preventing water from rushing to the channels and filling them up after each rainstorm. It is nature's way of preventing floods.

When rain causes flooding

A river channel is large enough to carry away the water that normally seeps in through the beds and banks. Periods of very bad weather (**storms**) often produce very heavy rainfall and it cannot all soak into the ground. When this happens water flows over the soil surface and rushes to the rivers quickly filling the channels. Once the channels are full, any more water floods out onto the surrounding landscape.

In winter, floods often occur when there is a long period with only moderate rain. There are no growing plants to suck up the moisture and the soil gets wetter and wetter. Some of the water will slowly seep away, but over several weeks the soil will often fill up. You can usually tell this because the soil feels spongy underfoot. When soil has filled with water, further rain runs quickly over the ground surface and into rivers where it is likely to contribute to a flood.

Melting snow

A total of three feet of newly fallen snow contains a depth of about 4 1/2 inches of water. With each new snowfall, more and more water is built up on the land surface.

In many parts of the world snow falls throughout the winter and at least three feet may have built up before the spring thaw.

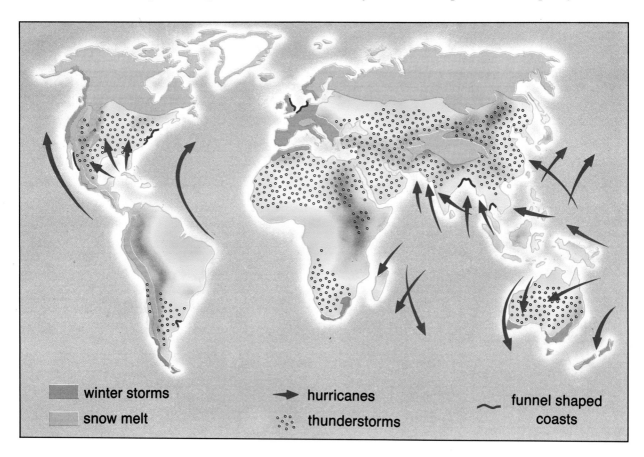

winter storms
snow melt
hurricanes
thunderstorms
funnel shaped coasts

▲   *Areas of the world where flood disasters are common.*

▲ *When this bridge in Wales was washed away, the train and its passengers were thrown into the swirling flood waters.*

The cold of winter also freezes the soil so that it becomes hard as rock and cannot absorb water.

Spring thaws usually come quickly to areas that have cold snowy winters, and it is not uncommon for a whole winter's snow pack to melt within a couple of weeks. With the soil still frozen almost all the melted snow flows off over the ground surface and floods are very common.

City floods

Cities are often the cause of floods. This is because the network of storm sewers and drains is designed to carry the rainwater to the rivers as quickly as possible. Very little water can seep into the soil. Large cities may send far more water to a river than it would receive naturally, so the chances of flooding are increased considerably.

Ocean floods

Ocean floods occur when storms blow onshore and pile ocean water against the coasts. In some places the coast forms a shape like a funnel. Storms often trap water into these areas, pushing it into a smaller and smaller area and forcing the water level to rise higher and higher. If the coast is very low-lying flooding frequently follows.

Why floods cause disasters

When a flood causes a disaster, it is nearly always because people put themselves at risk either intentionally or by accident. For example, in areas that are normally dry—the deserts and semi-deserts—rain is rare, but it always occurs in **cloudbursts.** Then most of the water rushes across the surface to give flash floods—the most dangerous kind of all. A river channel can be dry one moment and contain a raging torrent the next. Many people have been killed by such events because they do not understand the danger.

River Flood

Most of us like to be beside a river, to jump between half-submerged stones, to fish, or just to sit and listen to the sounds of the water. However, when a river swells with flood waters, when it turns muddy brown and its surface turns oily and thick, then a river bank is no longer a safe place to be.

Rocky Mountains

campers and houses
on narrow floodplain

Big Thompson
River

▶ *The flood happened in a part of the Rocky Mountains where giant clouds are held up against the mountain range. This diagram shows how the water from the storm was funneled into the Big Thompson Gorge.*

8

It is not always easy to know when a flood will come. On a summer vacation, for example, the weather is expected to be good. No one thinks of storms and floods. So when they do occur, it can be a recipe for disaster, as it was along the Big Thompson River at the end of July 1976.

The Big Thompson

The Big Thompson River cascades down from the Rocky Mountains in the state of Colorado. It is a beautiful and spectacular part of the country, and a favorite vacation area with people who want to walk in the mountains or fish for trout in the river. Along the river banks there are many campsites and vacation homes.

thunderstorm

There are also the homes of people who live permanently in the area, working in shops, for the forest service, and for tourists.

The Big Thompson has cut a very steep-sided valley and most people have had to build their homes on the small amount of flat land by the river. Campers and vacationers enjoy being by the river. However, the steep-sided valley provides very little room for the water to spill over when the river floods. There is no **flood plain** for the river to spill onto; there is no room for water to be stored so that it can slow down. Instead, the flood water is held in a small space and its speed is hardly slackened at all.

The flood begins

On this particular late July night the weather was quite bad. In the afternoon hot air currents containing huge **thunderstorms** had drifted northward from the Gulf of Mexico. One of these thunderstorms was a giant, towering more than 8 miles into the sky. As the storm reached the Rockies the huge bulk of the mountains held the cloud fast. The storm came to a halt over the Big Thompson Valley, releasing almost 10 inches of rain within six hours. This was several times the amount expected to fall in the whole month!

The soil could not soak up the torrential rain for more than a few minutes. Soon the rain began flowing over the soil surface. Within an hour from the beginning of the storm, water was rushing down the steep hillsides, reaching the river banks and pouring into the rapidly swelling channel. Meanwhile, all the vacationers were huddled in their tents or protecting themselves against the rain. As the storm advanced, darkness fell and it became impossible to see exactly what was happening on the hillsides. Forest rangers reported heavy rainfall but there was no easy way for the emergency services to predict how much flooding to expect. The rangers and the police were aware that the river level was rising at an alarming speed.

▲   *This house was torn from its foundation during the flood. It ended up straddled across a bridge many hundred of feet downstream from the place it was built.*

The police were told to begin to make the tourists aware of the danger. The local radio station began to forecast a worsening situation and the chance of flooding. Most people by the river did not take the warnings seriously, and even those who tried to take precautions were not able to do much before disaster struck.

The reason for the flood wave

Because the shape of the valleys in the Big Thompson area tends to gather all the streams together, all the waters from the mountain streams arrived together at the head of the deep, narrow Big Thompson Gorge. The gorge is the only route through the mountains. Every stream that fed water to the head of the gorge that evening was bursting its banks. It was simply impossible for all the water to get through the gorge fast enough without the water level rising dramatically.

As water piled up at the head of the gorge the scene changed too quickly for any of the emergency services to act. The water rose so fast that within minutes the water level had changed from 6 1/2 feet to 23 feet. When it reached this height the river changed its character and flowed in an uncontrollable surge of water called a **flash flood.**

The flood wave strikes

Although the flood wave lasted only a few hours, it brought with it a trail of death and destruction. The water came through the gorge rather like a sled on a bobsled run. On the outside of the bends it rode high up onto the valley wall, leaving the inside almost untouched; then it changed sides to ride up on the next bend.

The speeding water contained an enormous amount of energy. The bed and the banks of the channel were stripped; pebbles and even boulders were picked up from the valley floor and tossed along in the tumbling water. Full-grown trees toppled from the lower slopes of the gorge into the torrent, their roots undermined by the

◀ *This aerial view shows the way the houses in the Big Thompson Gorge became part of the riverbed during the flood. Boulders and gravel cover all the gardens.*

▼ *The flood carried away a large section of the interstate highway. The twisted remains of a water pipe lie stranded beside one of the road supports.*

rushing water. The water was so powerful the trees were carried along just like matchsticks.

The power of the water also allowed it to rip out a new channel along the floor of the gorge. As the bends in the old channel were cut through, the river path straightened and the water flowed even faster. Nothing could stand in its path now.

How the people fared

The luckiest people were in houses or tents on land on the inside of the gorge bends. Although homes and campsites were flooded, there was relatively little damage or loss of life. The main force of the river pushed against the outer bends and carried campers, tents, cars, homes, and bridges before it. A long section of the main interstate highway was ripped up, tossed into the gorge, and ground into small pieces. The supports carrying a huge water pipeline across the gorge buckled and broke. The pipe collapsed and water poured out, adding yet more to the flood.

Because there had been no time for the park rangers to organize an **evacuation,** when the people in the valley realized they were in danger, there was no time to escape and nowhere to go. A few people managed to scramble just far enough up the rocky

slopes to save their lives. However, for most people there was no escape from the terror of the water. When it was all over the police counted 139 bodies, collected the wreckage of 438 automobiles, and estimated the damage at $36 million. A vacation had been turned into a disaster.

Coastal Flood

Many people like to live beside the ocean on low-lying land. By doing this they put themselves at risk of high **tides** and lashing waves. Some of the greatest disasters from flooding happen at the coast.

▼ *This map shows how the North Sea basin behaved like a giant funnel as water was driven south by gale force winds during the fierce storm of 1953.*

Why coastal floods happen

Sea levels change as the moon makes its journey around the earth. Each day the moon's gravity pulls on the earth, causing two high tides. The sun also produces tides, but these change over a month, rather than a day. From time to time the tides produced by the sun and moon occur together giving a higher tide than normal. This is called the spring tide. High tides can cause floods.

During a storm, the winds push water ahead of them, forcing the water up against the land. This, too, can cause a flood.

A third reason for floods along the coast is the shape of the coast itself. Some

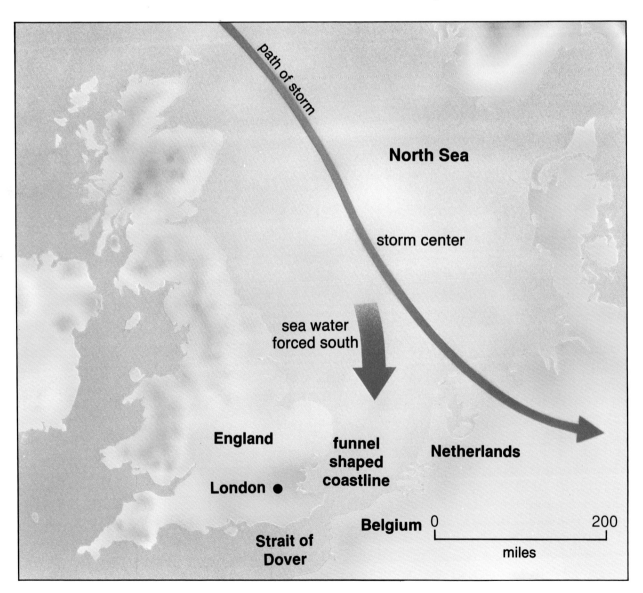

► *This is one of the largest dikes in the world. It is the Afluitsdijk, in the Netherlands, and it stretches for 20 miles across a large inlet near Amsterdam. It is all that keeps a huge fertile area from being flooded.*

◄ *This is what happened to coastal areas in 1953 when the dikes were broken in many places. It is difficult to tell the sea (right) from the land. Repairing the dikes and draining the land took many months.*

coasts have funnel shaped inlets. When a storm pushes water into an inlet that gets narrower toward the land, the extra water is squeezed into a smaller and smaller space. This forces the water level to rise. Sometimes storms force the level of the ocean in these inlets higher than the level in the rivers. When this happens the flow of water in river channels is reversed and water actually flows upstream!

When all three effects come at the same time, ocean levels can rise to be many feet higher than normal. Just such a combination of events caused the disastrous flooding along the shores of the North Sea in 1953.

The North Sea disaster of 1953

The coasts of the Netherlands, Belgium, northern France, and eastern England all have two things in common: they face the North Sea, and they are very low lying. Some land that has been reclaimed from the sea is below normal sea level and large walls called **dikes** are all that keep the sea out.

People have reclaimed the land because it has very fertile soil. In eastern England the lowest land is in East Anglia and is called the **fens**. In Belgium, the Netherlands, and northern France there are even bigger areas of reclaimed land, which are called **polders.** Most areas are protected by dikes, although many dikes are old and not very high. In other places the only protection from coastal floods is the natural line of sand dunes.

The North Sea is shaped like a funnel. Only the Strait of Dover between England and Belgium stops it from being completely closed at the south end. In winter most strong winds blow from the north, pushing water toward the narrow end of the sea.

On the night of the storm in 1953, the weather forecasters knew what to expect and warnings were given. "Evacuate all low-lying land, take the animals to places of safety, and look out for your lives." However, the night was pitch black, the storm was raging and, for many people near the coast, high land was many miles away.

Some people could do nothing but sit it out. It was to be a night they would remember for the rest of their lives. It was also a night that was going to influence what governments did for the next 30 years.

The flood strikes

Worst affected were the places near the narrowest part of the "funnel." Here the water level was more than 18 feet above normal—about the height of a bungalow. The sea level rose over three feet in just 15 minutes.

The weight of water and the pounding of the huge waves was too much for some of the dikes. Some simply broke up and allowed water to burst through. In other places the water actually flowed over the top of the dikes. That night tens of thousands of square miles were flooded, hundreds of people died, many thousands of animals were drowned, and hundreds of thousands were made homeless.

▲ ▶ *The black and white photograph shows how close London came to disaster in 1953. Water from the Thames River stands on both sides of the embankment wall designed to keep floods at bay. In the background are the Houses of Parliament.*

The color photograph shows the same scene taken today. Notice how the wall has been made higher.

The flood threatens London

As the storm pushed water into the Thames **estuary** Londoners became worried. The Thames is a funnel-shaped estuary at the end of the North Sea funnel. Much of the city is also very close to sea level.

Some parts of the city were especially at risk. The subway is nearly all below sea level. Many factories near the river kept their goods on the ground floor. If the factories were flooded everything would be ruined. London was looking at the prospect of a huge disaster.

On the night of the storm, water rose higher and higher, lapping up to the top of the embankment wall that protects the city. Then it started to spill over. In one place the wall protecting London was broken by the weight of the water. Within minutes over a thousand houses in the east sector of the city were flooded.

Just as the water lapped to the top of the embankment right in central London, the water level stopped rising and the city was saved. It had been just a hair's breadth from disaster. If the wall in the city center had been seriously surpassed, one and a half million people would have suffered and the death toll might well have reached tens of thousands. As it was many factories that lined the banks of the Thames River nearer the sea were flooded out and their goods destroyed.

Disaster sweeps the Netherlands

Northern Belgium and the south of the Netherlands were worst hit. Here there were no high protective walls to guard miles upon miles of flat, low-lying land. The only protection was a line of natural sand dunes and low dikes. The sand dunes were no match for the violent storm. The water simply washed over them and then poured inland. Over 1,800 people lost their lives and 50,000 cattle were drowned. Even the great Netherlands city of Rotterdam was badly flooded. Over 300 miles of dikes were damaged and there were 67 major gaps. The cost was in the hundreds of million of dollars. Today, it would total nearly two billion dollars.

▼ *Two people evacuating their home in East Anglia the morning after the storm. They are using an old tin tub as a makeshift boat!*

Drowned Valley

Floods are not always caused by storms. Sometimes a **landslide** causes massive amounts of rock and soil to block a valley. When this occurs the disaster may only affect a small area, but to the people involved it is just as distressing and dangerous. In the example that follows, you will find that a natural disaster can also lead to the death of a whole community. In this case the authorities decided that it simply was not worth paying the cost of rebuilding on the same site.

▼ ► *This diagram shows how the landslide blocked the valley. It shows the maximum size of the lake and the location of Thistle.*

The landslide

Just south of Utah's Great Salt Lake lies the Wasatch mountain range. The mountain slopes are very steep and the whole area is likely to suffer from great landslides.

▼ *This map shows the location of Thistle and the landslide in the Wasatch Mountains.*

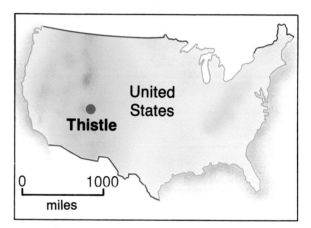

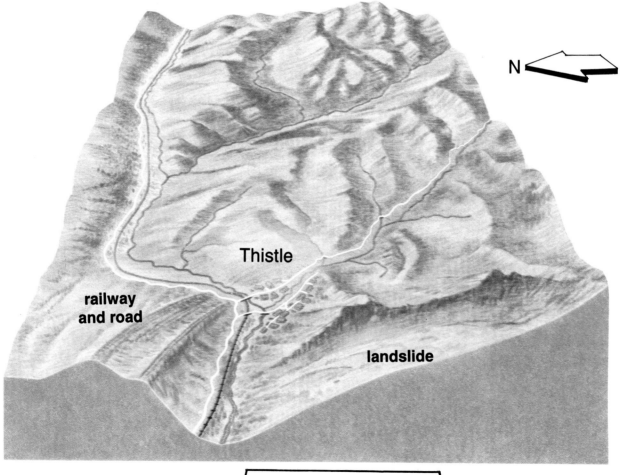

In spring 1985, an unusually large amount of melting snow and heavy rain seeped into the soils of the Wasatch Mountains. Near the top of one valley side, and overlooking the small village of Thistle, was a scarred area that bore the marks of a former landslide. The water seeped into the old landslide and set it moving once more. Without warning, the land began to slip, then flow. Within minutes millions of tons of soil and rock were flowing into the valley.

At Thistle, the valley is very narrow. A small river, an interstate highway, and the main railway line all squeeze into the bottom of the narrow valley. There was no room for a landslide as well as river, railway, and road. The slide quickly filled the floor of the valley and made a watertight seal across it. The dam created by the slide was 330 feet high! The railway and road were buried. This was enough of a disaster, but worse was to follow when the river was blocked.

The creation of Lake Thistle

Because the river water could not escape, it piled even higher behind the new dam. More snow melted and more rain fell, swelling the river. Within a short time the flood water had backed up so far that a new lake had been created. It was nicknamed Lake Thistle.

The people who lived in Thistle Village just upstream from the slide realized that disaster was at hand. Within days water was lapping around their homes and no one could do anything about it. Evacuation was the only answer. Day by day the water level kept rising until all the houses and many of the trees in the valley bottom were completely covered by the lake waters. Thistle had temporarily disappeared from the map!

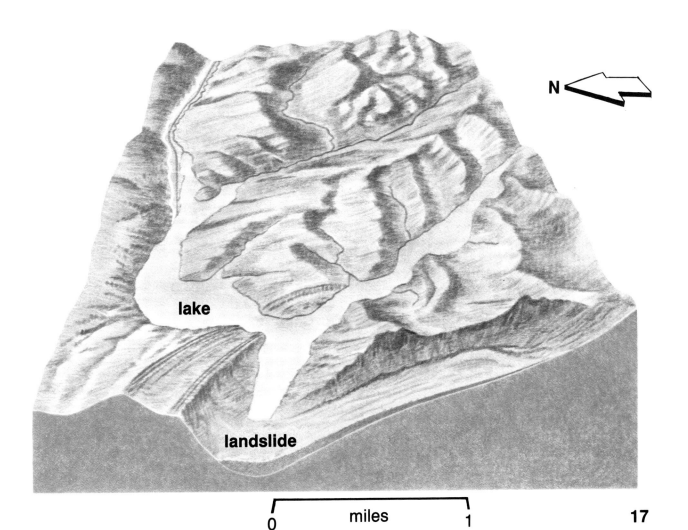

lake

landslide

N

0   miles   1

▲ *This house now lies abandoned even though Thistle Lake has been drained. It has more than 1 ½ feet of mud inside. Where there was once a garden, there is only mud. During the flood the water rose over the tree tops. The river flows on mud and its bed is over six feet higher than it used to be.*

Clearing the damage

The flood was a disaster for the people of Thistle, and it also completely stopped the flow of traffic to Salt Lake City from the east. The livelihoods of many people were at stake. The state authorities had to act quickly and build a new road and railway and try to drain the lake.

The landslide could not simply be bulldozed away. If this were done, more material from the mountain would slip into its place. The only solution was to reroute the railway through a special tunnel blasted into the hillside and take the road through a massive cutting. The lake could only be drained by blasting a relief tunnel through the valley wall. The cost would be enormous and the work would take years.

The relief tunnel took several months to dig. All of the time Thistle remained below the lake, its buildings full of muddy water. The mud in the water gently settled down, caking itself over the land and filling up the rooms of the houses. When the residents of Thistle saw their houses again, they discovered they were half full of mud. In some places the mud was so thick that the new riverbed was level with the floors of the houses. In one case the new river even ran past the tops of the windows!

The branch railway line from Black Rock Candy Mountain to Salt Lake City was badly affected. In one place all of the bridge supports had been washed away and the track hung crazily, like part of a roller coaster. In another place the track was buried by three feet of mud. Now that road transportation is much cheaper than rail, the branch railway will never be rebuilt.

◄　*The railway is unusable now because the bridge has been washed away. When the lake was at its height the water covered everything in sight.*

Living with disaster

Thistle is a good example of how a natural disaster can cause the death of a countryside village. Thistle was the home of a few people who had lived there all their lives. However, there were no shops and no factories or offices for people to work in. Thistle was a relic of a bygone age when most people lived on the land as farmers or laborers. When the flood came to the valley and drowned Thistle, it ended an era. It would have cost too much money to dig out the houses and make the village as good as new. Instead it was easier to move the villagers to other villages and towns.

Because the state has decided to let Thistle die, it has a deserted and almost haunted atmosphere. However, not everyone has been daunted by this disaster. Shirrell Young still visits the site of his former home in the pretty valley not far from the famous Black Rock Candy Mountain. He even has a sense of humor and has put up a sign to say that the settlement will rebuild. Not many people believe that though. Thistle is more likely to remain as a silent and curious monument to the disastrous results of a flood.

▲　*This photograph shows Shirrell Young, one of the inhabitants of Thistle who had lived in a house by the river for many years. After the flood there was nothing left of his house except for a few broken timbers. Shirrell intends to rebuild his house, although so far he has only managed to construct a makeshift bridge.*

19

How Nature Copes

A flood is a common part of nature. It is then that rivers are at their most powerful and that changes happen quickly in the landscape.

Each flood helps to carry away material that has built up since the last flood. This may be mud, sand, gravel, and boulders on the riverbed, it may be soil that has caved in from the banks of the river channel, it may be the material of a landslide, or it may be trees that have fallen over. Rivers do not usually have the energy to move any of these things. A flood that is a disaster for people is therefore a useful tool for nature.

Storing water in river channels

There are many places where water can be stored in the landscape. The largest of these **reservoirs** is called a lake, but some water can also be stored in river channels. River channels can help to store flood water because they are shaped in a succession of bends, or **meanders.** Meanders act as a brake on the water. Just as cars have to slow down to go around a bend, so water is slowed down as it goes around each meander. Because water cannot get through a meandering channel quickly, when there is a lot of water entering the channel it begins to fill up and acts as a kind of temporary reservoir. Flooding occurs only after the channel has been filled.

▼ *This diagram shows the many processes at work on a valley floor.*

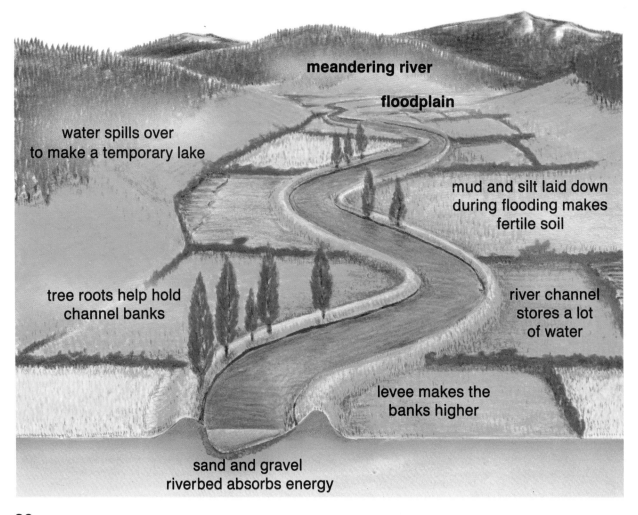

meandering river

floodplain

water spills over to make a temporary lake

mud and silt laid down during flooding makes fertile soil

tree roots help hold channel banks

river channel stores a lot of water

levee makes the banks higher

sand and gravel riverbed absorbs energy

◄ *Vegetation plays an extremely important role in reducing the rate of riverbank erosion. Here you see how the trees and shrubs are firmly holding the banks. Sometimes fallen trees make small dams, and this helps to hold back some of the flood waters.*

The floodplain

The floodplain is the flat land on either side of a river that becomes flooded whenever a river spills from its channel. Even a small river will have a floodplain somewhat wider than the channel. In many cases the floodplain is wide enough to contain all the meandering loops. Major rivers, such as the Mississippi, have floodplains that are many tens of miles across. The great size of a floodplain compared with a river channel means that it is the most important reservoir for flood waters.

Think of water on a floodplain as a large lake. It may be only a few inches deep, but its huge surface area means that the total amount of water stored is large. Water can be held on the floodplain lake until there is room for it in the channel once more, perhaps after a few days. When the level of water in the channel begins to fall, the water on the floodplain does not all rush back into the channel. Because the land is flat, flood water flows back slowly. Thus, the role of the floodplain is to even out the flood and stop the water level from rising too quickly. Deep flooding is more common in places such as the Rocky Mountains (page 8) where the rivers have not had time to cut a wide valley floor and form a flat floodplain.

► *In this flooded landscape almost the whole floodplain is under water. The levees show as dark-toned unflooded strips of land next to the river. Because the levees have been breached the flooding is very severe.*

How floods build floodplains

The floodplain is the key to flood control. To understand how floodplains are formed we first have to understand how a river shapes the floor of a valley.

Rivers are continually picking up and depositing **sediment.** At the height of a flood the river has far more energy than at any other time, and it picks up a lot of material from its bed and banks. Much of this water is carried onto the floodplain. Here it flows more slowly and much of the material is dropped. Each time a flood occurs another layer of sediment is deposited and the floodplain builds up.

Protecting against flood damage

Most floodplains are protected against flood damage by natural means more effectively than by the best defenses people could build. However, to watch the land flooding you would not think so. This is because you have to know how each piece of nature's jigsaw puzzle plays a role.

Just as people use sandbags to build a defensive wall against flooding, so nature uses the largest material it carries to build up the riverbanks. The coarse materials can

only be moved by fast river currents. As soon as water spills from the channel and slows down, the large materials settle out on the bank of the river. Each flood therefore raises the banks higher, gradually forming a natural wall known as an embankment, a dike, or a **levee.** Natural processes also have a way of being self-correcting, for the more the flooding, the more the banks build up.

Natural processes also work to reduce the damage from fast flowing flood water. As water spills over the floodplain it slows down and can no longer **erode.** In this way the erosion damage is limited to the channel banks. However, nature also has an efficient way of limiting channel damage.

A river carrying sediment is using up energy. The more it carries, the less surplus energy is available for the water to gain speed and cause more damage. As the river current swirls along the channel, material is eroded from the banks, using up energy and slowing down the water. At the same time, the wider channel can hold more water and is less likely to flood.

Nature uses its own means to trap a river in its channel. It relies on the fact that a river in flood can often change course, eroding its banks and forging a new pattern.

Flood-loving plants

Flood waters bring valuable materials to the floodplain. They spread a layer of fine particles called **silt** and mud which make up the floodplain soil. The waters are also rich in plant food called **nutrients.** Despite these advantages, only some plants can live successfully on floodplains. This is because water is never far from the surface and, during floods, plants can be submerged for many days at a time.

Some plants take advantage of the waterlogged ground and they thrive. These plants are also useful because as they grow their roots dig deep into the soil. These limit the damage caused by a flood because the stems of the plants trap mud and silt. The roots of trees growing by the side of a river keep the banks from eroding too quickly. Nature uses them as natural barriers to keep the channel stable.

All of these plants need to be able to stand up to the fierce attack of flooding water. Their branches and stems may sometimes break, but they are rarely washed away completely. With roots still firmly embedded in the soil it is not long before the plants are thriving again.

◄ *This river has forged a winding or meandering course across its floodplain. Although meanders are often cut through during floods, they rebuild quickly so that the winding course can slow the waters of the next flood.*

Why People Die

Many people are unaware of the hazards that can be caused by the forces of nature. On a fine summer's day, a place may look good to build a house on, but could be extremely risky at other times. Through long experience and over many generations, knowledge is gained to help plan which places are safe to build on and which places court disaster. The trouble comes when people arrive new to an area. They have no experience to rely on and they often make fatal mistakes.

▼ *This photograph shows the location of new vacation homes that could spell disaster if there were a flash flood. From the air it is easy to see that they have been built in the path of a river, but from the ground there is no simple way of recognizing the danger because the river channel is very shallow and wide and usually dry (see the photograph opposite).*

Ignoring nature's warnings

The story of Mr. and Mrs. Rosenberg may help you to understand how people come to put themselves in a dangerous position. They decided to buy a home in the Arizona desert. There are many new developments just right for vacation use in this state in the southwest. The Rosenberg's main home is in Los Angeles and they have never lived in the desert. They thought it would be relaxing.

As they toured around the countryside, the Rosenbergs saw a small new development on a piece of sloping land just below the edge of a mountain. It looked ideal. The slope of the land gave a superb view of the wide desert landscape. Then they noticed that the ground was very stony, and that many of the stones looked rounded and were quite large. Still, they thought, they hadn't intended to start a garden anyway.

The Rosenbergs bought their second home because they didn't know enough about rivers—or about the desert. The site of their home was on the **delta** of a desert

river. The attractive sloping land was the slope of the delta. Deltas are built up by rivers as they spill over their banks in time of flood. Large stones tell of former severe floods. The river where the Rosenbergs now have their second home does not flow very often and its channel is usually dry. The channel is wide and shallow and there is an asphalt road built across its bed. It is barely noticeable unless you are aware of the hazard. However, when there are storms in the nearby mountains the river can be struck by flash floods. The floods produce walls of water and carry away everything before them. Flash floods are not common; one may occur in this valley only once in a hundred years. But it only takes one to cause terrible destruction.

▶ *This hiker was following a trail along a dry stream bed five minutes before the photograph was taken. A thunderstorm in the nearby hills has turned the path to a swiftly flowing stream. This rapid change is typical of the desert.*

▼ *This road has been built across the delta of a desert river. The car is parked in the middle of a channel that sometimes carries a raging torrent. Homes built near this site could be destroyed by a flash flood.*

Tsunamis

People near the ocean sometimes die when they are caught by severe storm waves and coastal flooding. The worst kind of flooding comes with a **tsunami.**

If an **earthquake** happens beneath the ocean, the ocean floor shakes, setting waves in motion as if a giant pebble had been thrown into the water. The waves then spread out in all directions until they reach some far-off coast. A giant wave like this is called a tsunami.

Tsunamis can travel at terrific speed. Out in the deep water of the Pacific Ocean they may travel at over 375 miles per hour—the same speed as a jet plane. However, when they reach the shallow water near a coast they change speed and shape dramatically. Because they cannot keep moving forward, they rear up into towering giants sometimes over 80 feet high. Since these waves are too big to break they surge onto the land causing extensive flooding and often washing away people and houses that are in their path.

There is no natural warning from a tsunami—no bad weather or strong winds to warn of possible danger. Because the earthquake occurs so far away, no ground shocks are felt either. You can be sitting on the beach watching a calm sea and the next moment a freak tsunami wave can rush in before you have the chance to escape.

In the United States warnings of possible tsunamis are given when an undersea earthquake is detected. However, this has caused many people to rush to the coast to watch the wave, actually increasing their chances of being hurt or even killed.

▼ *In 1964 a tsunami was set in motion by an Alaskan earthquake. The force of the waves carried these ships onshore and wrecked cars parked by the coast.*

A greater risk of disaster

The people most at risk from flood disaster are the urban poor, especially in the **developing world**. They often live in low-lying areas and by rivers or on deltas, for these are the places that the better off choose not to live. In Guayaquil, Ecuador, for example, about 60 percent of the population live in **squatter** communities built over tidal land near the sea. They are thus likely to suffer from coastal flooding as well as river flooding.

In Bangladesh most of the country's 85 million people live on the Ganges Delta. This is an extremely crowded country and it is very difficult for young people to find new land and make a living. Often the only places open to them are the tidal mudflats that the river is still building out into the Bay of Bengal. Even under normal conditions they are barely above sea level. When a **cyclone** brings high storm tides

▲ *Jakarta, the capital city of Indonesia, is one of many developing world cities built over tidal land by the sea. In the foreground you can see slum housing built on low ground beside the river or on stilts right over the water. In the distance the modern office buildings are built on higher, less flood-prone land.*

from the Bay of Bengal, the results are nothing short of disastrous. No wonder so many people have been killed in this country in recent years. In May 1985 a cyclone washed over 6,000 people from these mudflats and they were drowned. Yet despite this tragedy, people were quick to start farming on the mudflats as soon as the storm was over and the floods had subsided. After all, they have nowhere else to go. They feel it would be as well to take their chances with the flood rather than face starvation.

Great Disasters

Floods are second only to droughts in the world scale of disasters. On average floods affect about 20 million people a year. The impact of a flood on countries throughout the world varies enormously. Some countries are particularly liable to suffer. On top of the list is China followed by Bangladesh in recent years.

The developing world suffers

In the table on this page you can see the world's great flood disasters. Clearly China stands out as the most flood-prone, but you will see that other countries of the developing world have also suffered greatly. The table shows how Bangladesh on the Ganges Delta has lost many people in recent years. As populations grow rapidly in these countries and more and more people crowd onto flood-prone land, it is certain that the world will see more and greater flood disasters than ever before.

China's rivers

China is the most disaster-prone country in the world. Because it has so many people (about 1.2 billion, or a quarter of the world's population) any disaster also affects very large numbers. In 1954, for example, a flood required the evacuation of at least ten million people.

China has many rivers that can and do cause seasonal flooding. Foremost among these are the two giant rivers; the Yangtze, which brings disaster to southern China, and the Huang He which often brings disaster to the north of the country.

Date	Type of Disaster	Country	Numbers Killed
1824	river flood	Soviet Union	10,000
1876	cyclone	India	200,000
1881	typhoon	Indonesia	300,000
1882	cyclone	India	100,000
1883	tsunami	Indonesia	37,000
1887	river flood	China	1-2 million
1889	dam failure	United States	2,200
1896	tsunami	Japan	27,000
1900	hurricane	United States	7,000
1911	river flood	China	100,000
1931	river flood	China	3 million
1931	river flood	Bangladesh	2,000
1938	river levees broken	China	500,000
1953	storm	NW Europe	2,000
1963	cyclone	Bangladesh	22,000
1963	dam overtopped	Italy	2,000
1967	dam failure	India	200
1970	cyclone	Bangladesh	500,000
1972	dam failure	United States	242
1976	river flood	United States	139
1977	cyclone	India	15,000
1981	river flood	China	3,000
1986	cyclone	Bangladesh	200,000

The Huang He River has killed more people than any other single feature of the Earth's surface. People have been channeling it, draining it, and building levees along it for over 4,000 years. In spite of their efforts, in 1887 the river still flooded, killing between one and two million people. The exact number is unknown. Although many died directly by drowning, many more died later of starvation because their crops had been destroyed by the flood. In 1931 the river flooded again—killing up to three million people.

Over the past 2,000 years the levees have been breached by the river over 1,500 times. In 1938, however, the enormous levees were broken by the Chinese to try to stop the invading Japanese armies. It did hold back the Japanese—but also killed 500,000 Chinese because the farmers were given no warning.

Even today the toll of disasters shows no signs of diminishing. In 1981, the Szechuan province was hit by flooding that affected ten million people.

▲   *This picture shows workers cutting a channel into the Huang He riverbed. In times of flood, water would stretch to the horizon.*

▼   *This Bangladeshi woman waits waist deep in water for a rescue boat to arrive.*

Great disasters of the future

The Huang He River is also called "China's sorrow" because of the number of people it has killed. It gets its other nickname, "Yellow River" from the vast amount of yellow silt it carries. This is brought down from the soft silt hills that cover much of the northern part of China. The silt, which may become as much as 40 percent of the entire flow, is continually dropped on the riverbed, so the river is steadily rising above the surrounding land. In the last 40 years the bed has risen by six feet. For much of its journey across the vast Yellow Plain, the river is now 30 feet above the surrounding landscape. It is only held in check by building the levees ever higher.

Cutting trees in the hills has made the situation far worse. **Deforestation** began early last century when trees were cut for fuel and building. But the major change came in 1958 when the leader of the Communist Party in China, Mao Tse Tung, encouraged every family to make steel in their own backyards using charcoal as a fuel. Later, yet more forests were cleared to make room for extra farmland.

▼ *This map shows the huge area drained by the Huang He River. The yellow area downstream of the Sanmenhsia Dam is most likely to flood.*

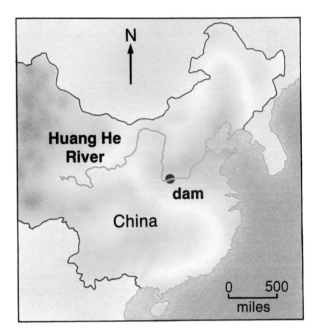

▼ *The Sanmenhsia Dam was built across the Huang He to help prevent flooding. It has become so choked with silt in the last 30 years that the gates have to be kept open in times of flood and the dam does not reduce flooding at all.*

▲   *The Woodburn flood in New South Wales, Australia, was a great financial disaster because so many homes were affected. Inside each lies thousands of dollars worth of damaged carpets, furniture, and other goods.*

With no tree roots to open up the soil and allow water to soak in, rain now reaches the river faster than ever. It also brings more silt than in the past, causing the riverbed to rise and requiring the levees to be built up even faster. Unless conservation measures become effective in China, it will not be long before the world's greatest disaster is once more China's sorrow.

The great cost of flooding

Flooding disasters in the developing world can cost millions of lives. The tragedy is in terms of people rather than property because those who suffer are poor and have few possessions. In the developed countries the reverse is true. A great flood is unlikely to cost many lives, but many homes and workplaces will be flooded and there will inevitably be massive insurance claims by the people affected. Thus, in the modern world, a small-scale flood that may affect only a restricted area of a country can easily be a great financial disaster.

Emergency

When a disaster hits an area or a country many people will need help. But to be effective, those who come to help in an emergency must be clear about what to do. This means that the rescue teams must have prepared a flexible plan.

The scale of the problem

The first thing to do in any emergency is find out the scale of the problem. After the flood has occurred, as soon as weather permits, inspection teams must be airlifted by helicopter to critical places; to hospitals, to schools, and to nursing homes. These teams all report back to a central control by radio, as soon as they can. At the same time more helicopter squads of police or military

► **Small boats are used by the fire and rescue departments in Brisbane, Australia, to rescue people trapped in the upper floors of their flooded homes.**

forces go and take a bird's-eye view of the disaster. Their job is to note which places seem in most difficulty and where the biggest areas of damage are. They must report back in just the same way as they do for traffic reports every day. The more low key they can keep the situation the better. If everyone is well drilled the rescue can be carried out efficiently, without panic.

Setting up a control center

It may take many hours before the scale of the disaster will be known because the effects of floods vary enormously. River floods may just leave people stranded; tsunamis may leave many thousands dead and injured. In a disaster involving dead and injured, top priority must be given to the injured. A temporary landing pad for the helicopters must be set up away from the disaster zone. An airport is often a good place to use as the hub of operations for the rescue, but there are other possibilities, such as the lawns of a hospital.

The next stage is to be able to cope with the massive number of injured people. Ordinary hospitals won't be able to cope with so many injured people even if their buildings remain undamaged. A field hospital made of medical tents must be set up on dry land. The huge flat spaces at airports can also be used for a hospital, storing supplies, and for other purposes.

The people caught up in the disaster will be wet and often shocked. They will need shelter and food. If the disaster is on a small scale, local schools and church halls make good bases for temporary kitchens and places to stay. A large-scale emergency will need tented villages.

Cleaning up

At the end of a flood disaster there are two problems to overcome. First, there is a vast amount of cleaning up to do. All the mud and other debris that the water brought along will have to be cleared out, too. Often clearing the debris is a much harder job than pumping out the water.

Some things can be done quickly. Water that has flooded into basements and cellars can be pumped out by the fire department. Nevertheless, removing surface water is only the start. For example, all the furniture will be soaked through. Heaters will have to be used to speed up drying or the furniture may rot. Also electrical wires that are wet are dangerous.

◀ *The floodwaters that covered this street have subsided, but the street, the grass, and the inside of the houses, are all caked with thick red-brown mud.*

▼ *Rivers in flood often erode their banks, undermine bridge supports, and cut into roads. This may disrupt communications and make it difficult to reach people with all the provisions they need.*

Plaster will have become saturated on the walls and it may have started to dissolve; wallpaper will have begun to peel off the walls. To dry all this out costs a great deal of money and power will probably have failed as electricity will have been shorted out by the flood waters. Nothing can be done until electricity is restored.

Clinging mud

Many rivers carry very large amounts of sediment during a flood. As the flood waters recede and the level falls, the water speed slackens and there is not enough energy to carry away all the sediment. At this point the material is deposited, mainly as a glue-like coating that cakes itself onto all surfaces.

Mud gets into everything. It is almost impossible to get it out of furnishings even after they have dried out. Thus mud rather than water damage often costs most to rectify. Mud also clogs up roads and buries crops, often to such a depth that the plants are killed. Mud gets into water pipes and fills them up, it gets into drains and blocks them. Even scraping or hosing mud from the streets is a major task.

Effects of erosion

Rivers in flood can cut into their banks and often produce completely new channels. Houses placed near riverbanks may thus have their foundations undermined. They may need shoring up or, if the damage is too severe, they may have to be demolished completely.

Rivers may well have destroyed bridges and other structures. All these structures will have to be rebuilt, with new designs that can cope better with flood conditions. Some protective measures may also be taken, such as building up river-banks or building protective walls.

The developing world

The world's biggest flood disasters happen in the developing world. In poorer countries, governments do not have many funds in reserve for a disaster, and will often need to look to the wealthier nations for extra help. However, providing emergency help may not be that simple.

Suppose you were on a relief team going in to help with a flood disaster just after it has happened. How could you help? Stop and think for a moment. What would these people normally be doing? Do they need blankets or your old clothes in a tropical climate? Do they like the sort of food you eat, and will it upset their stomachs? (After all, when we go abroad foreign food sometimes disagrees with us, so why not the other way around?).

A great many homes will have been damaged. Emergency help could include the building of better homes, but those homes have to be suitable. How are these people going to repair their better homes in years to come? They can't afford to buy expensive materials. They might expect people to come back and help them again. When the emergency relief teams have gone the people must be able to manage on their own again.

Emergency help is vital. It will save lives and be of great comfort. Most emergency help is needed by the poorer countries. But that help must be given with care or yet another disaster may develop in spite of the best of intentions.

▼   *Flood disasters leave many people homeless and without any means of feeding themselves. Here food is being distributed from a boat to people caught in a flood disaster in Bangladesh.*

Be Prepared

What is the best way to prepare for flood disasters? It is very difficult to generalize because some countries are in parts of the world more liable to floods than others. However, if we take a large country such as the United States over a 12 month period, it is possible to see the variety of floods. This will help us to see what preparation needs to be done.

Few parts of the United States escape some form of flooding during any year, although most of it occurs in just a few small areas. A typical year will see floods from hurricanes, landslides, heavy rain, and melting spring snows.

In the United States there are not usually many deaths because there are good warning systems and rescue services. However, people cannot move their homes when a flood occurs and so the amount of property damage can be very high. In a recent year damage of over $300 million was claimed from flood disasters.

Taking care with land use

People can make their own floods worse if they don't think through how they use the land. Being prepared means understanding how natural processes work.

Nature relies on water being able to soak into the soil. Tree roots help to break up the soil and allow water to soak in. When trees are cut down the water does not soak in as well and more water runs over the surface to rivers.

◄ The land shown here has been planted in strips along the contours of the hill. Any water that runs over the surface of the gold strips (grain) is trapped in the green strips in between (grass), where it sinks into the soil. In this way little surface water rushes to streams to cause flooding elsewhere.

Any settlement covers some of the ground with waterproof surfaces such as streets and pavements. Most of the water falling onto roofs of houses is collected in gutters and then funneled into drains. Very little rainwater is allowed to soak into the ground, making it reach the rivers even more quickly. Quite often, too much reaches the river channels at the same time. In this way people are often the cause of their own floods.

In the industrial countries farmers are often encouraged to drain their hill lands to provide better grass for their animals. Farmers bury drains in the fields, thereby carrying water quickly to rivers. This may be good for the fields but it can be a disaster for lowland city dwellers who may get flooded much more often. People in the lowlands have to be prepared for the floods caused in this way or they must persuade farmers to conserve their land more wisely.

Controlling flood damage

How can flood damage be controlled? The first thing to understand is how nature uses the land. A floodplain is made by a river, and there is nothing more certain than that the river will use it from time to time. So the worst possible use of floodplain land is to build houses on it, since during a flood not only property but also the lives of residents will be at risk.

Every city needs parks, sports fields, and parking lots. None of these would be damaged by flood water, and open spaces also give a breath of fresh air to a congested riverside city. Open space and recreation should be the first choice for the floodplain nearest the river, because this is the area most likely to flood.

If people *must* build on a floodplain they will have to protect themselves. Factories and warehouses can be located in the more flood-prone sites. These buildings can be put on stilts and the ground floors used as parking lots. (Cars are easily evacuated in a flood.)

Building to control floods

Planning ahead is the cheapest and most reliable way of being protected from a flood. However, in places that are already built up there are other much more expensive ways of preparing for a flood. City authorities can decide to build a protective wall or levee around the main built-up area to keep the floodwaters out. New Orleans in the south has such a levee to keep the Mississippi River from overflowing its banks and flooding the city.

◄ This is the Thames Barrage in London. It is one of the biggest civil engineering works ever undertaken on a river. In this photograph you can see only part of the barrier; the gates lie flat on the riverbed. When a coastal flood threatens, the gates are raised and the river is then sealed from a tidal surge.

▲ *Anything blocking or narrowing the channel makes it more difficult for the water to flow away. The width of the Thames River in London has been reduced to less than two-thirds of its natural size and it has to be protected with a riverbank wall (called the embankment).*

Instead of trying to keep the water out, it is possible to feed the extra water into specially dug flood relief channels. Usually dry, these channels allow water to flow off rapidly. Los Angeles has such large channels that filmmakers use them for car chases and even fly aircraft along them!

The protection methods described so far only work for individual cities or towns. However, there are many valleys where all of the settlements are liable to flood. It would be wastefully expensive, unsightly, and inconvenient to build a levee around each one. And the effects would still not protect the farmland in between. It is possible to provide protection to many settlements in a valley by holding back that part of the river flow that would have caused the floods. This can be done by building a dam across rivers that pose a threat. Normally the reservoir behind the dam is kept at a low level. When heavy rain occurs water is held back in the reservoir, then released slowly after the danger has passed. Huge dams and reservoirs have been built in many countries.

◄ *There is little that can be done in some places except to warn people about the risks and hope they can take care of themselves.*

▼ *An artists's impression of the ways flooding can be reduced in an urban area and at the same time improve the environment.*

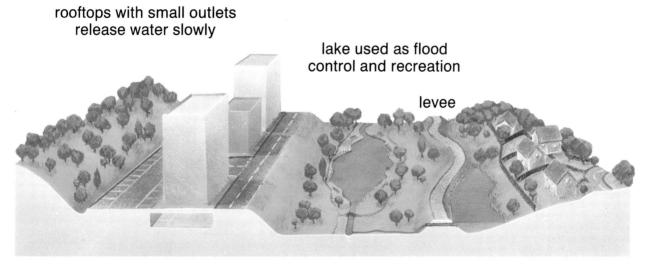

rooftops with small outlets
release water slowly

lake used as flood
control and recreation

levee

only parking lots
below flood level

Improving the environment

The diagram above shows how people can plan to protect themselves from a flood and at the same time improve their environment. The artificial lake has been formed by damming the stream. In times of high stream flow the lake will simply store much of the excess and prevent flooding in the valley. The lake and the floodplain are kept as open space. This reduces the risk of flooding damage and gives a place for people to enjoy.

The houses are protected from flooding by a small levee. Storm water from the house drains goes into a pond behind the levee with only a small outlet pipe to the stream. This slows down the water on its way to the stream.

Outside the office buildings the ground is made of special concrete blocks designed to allow water to sink into the soil. The tops of the office buildings have been designed to store water, their outlet drains are small so that they release water slowly.

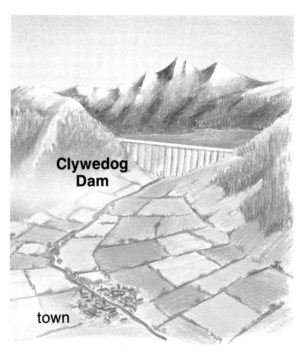

Clywedog
Dam

town

▲ *The Clywedog Dam on the headwaters of the Severn River in central Wales has been designed to hold back water during a period of stormy weather and prevent the flooding of many towns downstream.*

Waiting for Disaster

More and more flood disasters are being created by people. Here is a story from the Indian Himalaya Mountains that shows how dramatic the effect can be.

The story of Surya

Surya knows only too well how the land has changed in his lifetime. When he was a young boy the mountains were still covered in the dark green of giant pine trees. Even the steepest Himalayan slopes had a protective cover of trees. Of course, at this time nobody knew that the trees were protecting the land. It never occurred to people in their mountain homes that clearing away the trees might bring disaster to the city dwellers of Calcutta over 600 miles away. However, there were many pressures on the land that Surya knew so well. His family, and the families of his friends, were all increasing in numbers. Each family had to support itself and needed more land for more animals to graze. They also needed wood for their fires and for building their homes. So the farmers of the Himalayas began to cut down many trees, so quickly that new trees could not grow fast enough to replace the old ones.

▶ *Surya sits by the wood fire on which he is cooking his supper. He had to travel half a day's journey on horseback to find the wood.*

Changes in land use

Over the years, the farmers started to notice that something very curious was happening. Where the land had been heavily grazed the grass could not hold the soil in place. Every time it rained the water ran over the surface instead of soaking into the soil. Bare patches started to appear on the slopes. The stream waters, once so clear, were now often a muddy brown because they were full of soil from the eroded slopes. The precious mountain soils were being carried away. Each year more and more water flowed over the surface where before it had soaked into the ground. Floods started to be more common in the valleys.

Then one day the first of the loggers from the lowlands arrived. They had been given permission to cut down some of the trees and carry them away for making timber. But the scale of their operations was much greater than anything Surya had witnessed before. Soon the forests were disappearing at an alarming rate, and the more they disappeared the more often the floods came.

Surya found that the land left bare by the loggers was good to graze his animals. Unfortunately the animals ate both the grass and the small saplings that would eventually have grown into new trees. In this way the grazing stopped the trees from regrowing and kept the mountains permanently bare of forest.

▲ *The flocks of sheep that are now commonplace in the Himalayas prevent the tree saplings from growing.*

◄ *This is Surya's summer home in the mountains. As soon as the snows clear in spring, the animals are brought to the mountain pastures. You can see how heavy overgrazing has led to widespread bare patches on the slopes behind the huts.*

Hasari's story

In the city of Calcutta, more than 600 miles from where Surya lived, Hasari was a rickshaw puller. His home was a hut near the great Hoogley River which flowed through the crowded metropolis of ten million people. Hasari also realized that things were changing, although he did not know why. During recent monsoons, his poor slum hut had been flooded completely. On occasion he had had to seek safety on higher ground. However, since most of Calcutta is less than 30 feet above sea level, where could he and his family go?

A very difficult problem

Surya and Hasari were suffering from the deforestation of the mountains. In 1978 an Indian government survey showed that probably one person in 20 was at risk from flooding. India is a vast country. In that year between June and September alone, 46,000 villages were flooded and crops from eight and a half million acres were lost. In 1980

▲ *In the monsoon season it is common for areas in Calcutta to be flooded. These slum dwellings on the outskirts of the city are surrounded by floodwaters.*

▼ *People in the center of the city can find themselves walking to work for many days at a time through flooded streets. The shops have floors raised high to reduce the risk of losing their goods.*

floods washed over large parts of the northern plains and killed 1,800 people who lived by the rivers. Mud huts have little resistance to floodwater and many people died when their houses collapsed.

Flooding also mixes **polluted** river water with the water people have to drink. The disaster of being without a home can be made worse by the diseases people catch from drinking polluted floodwater. It is a great added expense to have to try to stop flooding and prevent water pollution.

Calcutta could only save itself from yearly disaster by building a large levee to keep the river waters at bay and by using large pumps to drain off surplus rainfall. However, the city is very poor and cannot afford this solution. The people of Calcutta can only expect greater and greater disasters in the years to come unless reforestation takes place in the Himalayas.

The way forward

The Indian government is trying to tackle the reforestation program. Success at replacing the forests of the Himalayas will bring benefits all the way down the river. Each town and city would not have to build its own levees, but could use the money saved on other vital projects. The way forward is to show the mountain people that they can gain from a tree saving campaign. Already there are some villages where the women are responsible for growing new trees. They achieve this by keeping more animals in pens, rather than letting them wander over the mountainside. The women then gather grass for the animals by cutting it in areas where saplings are growing. The women can cut all the green plants for the animals but leave the trees unharmed. The dung produced by the animals is then kept on the farm and spread on the soil. Dung is vital because, when it is dug into farmland it helps to hold the soil together, allowing rainwater to soak in and not run straight to the river. As the trees grow they are cut for wood, but immediately replaced with new saplings.

In this way people get as much wood as they want, including plenty of firewood. The animals get enough to eat and the soil is protected and made fertile again. The villages that have begun to adopt the new way of working are now much better off. The next task of the Indian government is to persuade all villages to adopt the same technique. Then people in the lowlands will not be experiencing disaster so often.

◀ **Buses plow their way through streets in the center of Calcutta. On many days the water level is higher than the wheels.**

Benefits of Floods

When flooding leads to so much disaster it is difficult to imagine that it can possibly bring any benefits. However, most towns and cities were built on floodplains because their founders thought the benefits outweighed the likelihood of occasional disaster.

Using the floodplain

As we have already seen, people can use the floodplain unwisely. This is because towns and cities have now grown up for uses different from those imagined by their founders. The people who founded Calcutta, for example, chose the site of a levee and welcomed the flooding because it made it easy to defend the new settlement.

The Nile floods

In the past people welcomed the flat land built up by centuries of flooding. The Nile River brought silt and nutrients to the parched lands of Egypt every year during the seasonal floods. People knew when the flooding would happen and moved away until it was over. Then they returned to plant seeds in the wet soil.

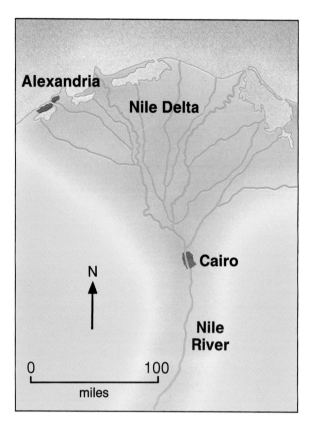

▲ **Egypt would be an unproductive desert without the Nile floods. For centuries, Egypt has managed to feed its people by farming the precious strip of land beside the river.**

▶ **This photograph shows how close the desert sands come to the floodplain of the Nile River. The men in the foreground are still in the desert, but they are looking over the green trees of Cairo's suburbs.**

The Nile was able to provide food for the people of Egypt over thousands of years, because of flooding. There was no need to put fertilizer on the fields because nutrients were replaced each year by the floods. It is only since the Aswan High Dam was built in the 1950s that the floods have stopped. Now farmers have to pay for fertilizer instead.

Higher up the Nile River, in the Sudan, there are tribes that still rely on the annual floods. One such tribe is the Dinka and they live near a huge swamp called the Sudd. Each year they follow the receding flood, to graze their cattle on the grass that has grown in the flooded soil. Without the annual flood, the Dinka could not find enough grazing land for their cattle.

New land from floods

Rivers carry the most sediment in times of flood. A great deal is stored on floodplains when the rivers overflow their banks. The remainder is carried down river and deposited in the sea to form a delta.

Deltas are nature's way of reclaiming new land. As each new flood spills over the delta, more material is deposited and the delta builds up. The Netherlands in northwest Europe is nearly all built on a delta that has been created by three rivers; the Rhine, the Meuse, and the Scheldt. Over ten million people now live on this delta.

Africa has some of the world's largest deltas. Egypt's second largest city, Alexandria, has been built on the edge of the Nile Delta, and much of the land is used for farming. The Nile Delta is spared the ravaging storms suffered by the Bangladeshi who live on the Ganges Delta. In Egypt millions of years of flooding have brought far more benefits than problems.

People who create floods

Throughout much of Asia people rely on rivers to bring fresh water to their rice fields. Many of them are built on the floodplains of large rivers, like the Mekong and Ganges. Rice needs a lot of water to grow and farmers have to build special walled fields which can be kept permanently flooded.

These **paddy fields** grow more food than any area of comparable size on Earth. Water is diverted from the rivers to flood these lands. Just as with the Nile floods, much of the fertilizer needed by the plants is brought with the water. Houses are built on stilts so that people can protect themselves in times of river floods. Here, just as in Egypt, people find more benefits than problems from flooding.

◄ *A farmer plows his paddy fields in preparation for a new season's planting. Rice needs flooded land to thrive.*

Glossary

cloudburst
the name given to an intense downpour of rain that begins suddenly. It is usually caused by a thunderstorm.

cyclone
an alternative name for a hurricane used in South Asia

deforestation
the complete removal of trees from an area. Deforestation can cause flooding, soil erosion, and even changes in climate.

delta
a large fan of coarse materials, such as sand and gravel, deposited by a river at the end of its course. It is made as the river splits up into several smaller channels which spread outward and help to make the fan wider.

developing world
countries that have not yet become fully industrialized and that do not have a wide range of health, water, and other facilities open to the majority of the people. In most developing countries the majority of the people work as farmers.

dike
a long earth bank designed to keep water from farmland. The earth bank is usually surfaced with stone to resist erosion.

disaster
a severe event that disrupts the normal lives of people

earthquake
a violent shaking of the ground surface due to forces within the Earth

erode
to wash away soil or riverbed and banks with the force of water

estuary
a wide inlet along the coast where a river reaches the sea

evacuation
an organized movement of people to get them clear of a danger zone

evaporation
the loss of water from the oceans or other wet surface to the air. Water in the air is called moisture.

fens
a name for low-lying marshy areas that are easily flooded

flash flood
a flood that happens within a few minutes, turning a dry channel into a raging torrent. The water then flows over the channel banks to flood the surrounding land. Most flash floods are produced by intense thunderstorms.

flood
unusually high level of water in a river or at the coast causing the water to spill over areas of the surrounding landscape that are normally dry

floodplain
the flat land on either side of a river channel that is covered with water when a river spills over its banks

landslide
a slide of loose rock and soil down a steep slope

levee
an earth bank by the side of a river that helps to keep river water from flooding across the landscape. It may be natural or constructed by people.

meanders
the bends in a river channel

moisture
water contained within the air as a gas. Moisture increases in the air when water evaporates from wet surfaces. Moisture is lost from the air when it condenses into cloud droplets.

nutrients
the chemical foodstuffs that plants absorb from rain and soil water

paddy fields
farmland used to grow rice in small fields. Each field is surrounded by small earth walls and flooded with water.

polder
a Dutch name for a low-lying area that would be flooded under natural conditions.

It is kept as dry farmland by continuously pumping out the water. Polders are surrounded with earth walls called dikes.

pollute
to spoil or poison the air, land, or water with waste, garbage, fumes, or noise. noise.

reservoir
a place where water is stored. Natural reservoirs are called lakes, but people often make reservoirs by building dams across river valleys. These are used to control the amount of water and thus prevent flooding.

sediment
the material carried by a river, either in suspension or by rolling and bouncing it along the bed. Clay, silt, sand, and gravel are all types of sediment. Clay particles are the smallest and gravel is the largest.

silt
fine material carried by a river, slightly smaller than sand

squatters
people who come to live on land without any legal right. Squatting is common in developing countries because many people don't have enough money to afford to rent or buy land.

storm
severe weather, usually consisting of strong winds and possibly heavy rain or snow

thunderstorm
an outburst of heavy rain or hailstones from a single cloud. Clouds that produce heavy rain are called cumulus clouds. They are often accompanied by lightning and thunder.

tide
the changing heights of the sea surface caused by the pulling forces of the moon and the sun

tsunami
a number of waves of water that are caused by an earthquake or volcanic eruption below an ocean floor. Each wave rushes forward at hurricane speed and arrives on coasts with no warning. So much water is contained in a tsunami that the waves flood up to one mile inland. A tsunami wave may be 25 feet high.

volcanic eruption
a sudden breaking out of material from within the Earth. A volcanic eruption normally begins with large amounts of ash, gas, and steam being thrown out.

▼ *This photograph gives a vivid impression of the torrential rain that falls during a monsoon.*

Index